The Writer's Revision Handbook

The Writer's Revision Handbook

Summary Points for Revising

by Blair Adams
with Joel Stein

ISBN-0-916387-27-5

Published by

TRUTH FORUM

2433 N. 43rd Street, Waco, Texas 76710

Printed in the United States of America

To help the writer, since that is his job, the teacher must enable the writer to see—partly by showing him how the [writing] betrays his distorted vision (as [writing], closely scrutinized, always will)—that his personal character is wanting.

Some writing and revision teachers feel reluctant to do this kind of thing, and people . . . with no burning convictions about writing or the value of getting down to bedrock truth . . . are inclined to be sympathetic. Nobody's perfect, they generously observe. But [we must be] impatient with such talk. Circus knife-throwers know that it is indeed possible to be perfect, and one had better be. Perfection means hitting exactly what you are aiming at and not touching by a hair what you are not.

John Gardner

Think of and look at your work as though it were done by your enemy.

Samuel Butler

A writer is unfair to himself when he is unable to be hard on himself.

Marianne Moore

There are two sorts of eloquence; the one indeed scarce deserves the name of it, which consists chiefly in laboured and polished periods, an over-curious and artificial arrangement of figures, tinselled over with a gaudy embellishment of words, which glitter, but convey little or no light to the understanding . . . . The other sort of eloquence is quite the reverse to this, and which may be said to be the true characteristic of the holy Scriptures; where the eloquence does not arise from a laboured and far-fetched elocution, but from a surprising mixture of simplicity and majesty, which is a double character, so difficult to be united, that it is seldom to be met with in compositions merely human.

Laurence Sterne

The vital difference between a writer and someone who merely is published is that the writer seems always to be saying to himself, as Stendhal actually did, "If I am not clear, the world around me collapses."

Alfred Kazin

Contents

Introduction 1

Summary Points for Revising
- General Points to Always Check 3
- Choosing the Best Word 3
- Cut Excess Words 8
- Clarity and Diction 9
- Right Verbs and Prepositions 11
- Right Modifiers 19
- Metaphors and Imagery 20
- Showing and Details 20
- Names 22
- The Sound of Words 23
- Sentence Structure 25
- Eliminate False Voice 33
- Continuity and Conjunctions 38
- Consistency 40
- General Structure 42

NOTES 45

BIBLOGRAPHY 51

Introduction

This booklet offers some concise points for refining your writing, points gleaned from dozens of handbooks, writing manuals and other sources, and from practical experience derived from writing steadily for almost two decades. While you can use this *Revision Handbook* independently of other instructional material, we suggest using it in conjunction with *Right Words: The Grace of Writing*. This *Handbook* will *not* teach you how to write, but it will help you to refine and revise what you've written. Proper revision in writing helps clarify, impact and persuade. It produces fruit in the same way that pruning a peach tree does. Life, however, must first course through the properly planted tree before pruning can benefit it, and the same holds true for writing. To produce a writing with life, turn to *Right Words*.

To revise your writing, acquaint yourself with the points in this *Handbook*; then check over whatever writing you're working on. (Note that the importance of a point is not proportionate to the length of its explanation; some central points take the least space.) The more familiar you become with the revision points, the more successfully you'll incorporate them into your own writing. While you check for these points, also watch for and change mistakes in grammar, punctuation, capitalization, consistency of format and spelling. In the first rereading, you will mainly concern yourself with precision and forcefulness of word usage and imagery. To perfect this requires acute concentration and care, but the result richly rewards the effort. Once you complete the polishing, you complete the writer's task, and the arduous but essential job of the proofreader (at least done once or twice by the writer) now takes over. We discuss the basic principles of punctuation, grammar and other elements related to proofreading in a separate study.*

Some of the following material reviews and summarizes points made in *Right Words*, although this booklet introduces many points not included there. Remember, here your emphasis is on *revision*, literally "seeing your writing again."

* See Truth Forum's *Clear Words: A Relational Approach to Grammar and Punctuation.*

Summary Points for Revising

General Points to Always Check

1. Don't slavishly follow any rule that causes awkward or confused writing. If the writing transmits real voice with clarity and power, you have the substance of what you're looking for.

2. You must have a clear understanding and feeling for what you want to say.

3. Speak to your reader.

4. Read your writing aloud, preferably to someone else. If you don't like its sound, rework it. If something is too turgid, dense, awkward, dead, rewrite it completely. Try a new free writing.

Choosing the Best Word

5. Use words accurately. "Have a point and make it by means of the best word."[1]

> The writer, consciously or not, writes for someone. He begins by being his own audience, in the sense of having to act toward himself like a demanding reader. His perpetual question is: do these words, does this paragraph, does the entire piece, suit my present purpose? The purpose at large is always the same: it is to be understood aright. Reader and writer have both wasted their time if mental darkness is the only result of their separate efforts. And—this is the

> very ethics of writing—the reader's part of the effort must never become a strain . . . .
>
> The adapting of words to needs, this goal of *suitability*, about which the writer continually challenges himself, naturally breaks up into a great many particular questions—is this the suitable term or form? the suitable order of ideas? the suitable length? and so on.[2]

6. Words carry all sorts of associations and secondary meanings, connotations that have "grown by usage around" their "core" meanings, or denotations.[3] Sacrifice those words that now have a confused meaning in the reader's mind, even if the dictionary definition or old usage matches your intention. For example, Barzun explains that *restive* once meant "stubborn." Even if you know this, you can't use this word in that sense, because it has now come to mean "impatient."[4]

Other words have changed in yet more fundamental ways than this because the very institutions, concepts, even nations to which the terms apply, have radically altered. When two people express a desire for "freedom," they may mean two radically different ideas. One may mean State-enforced social equality, while the other means the liberty to live without such State intrusions. Terms such as *justice*, *tolerance* and related words likewise carry diverse and often conflicting connotations in different people's minds today. Similarly, two people can each express a love for "America," but have radically counterposed notions of what this name stands for. You must know precisely what you mean when you use words, especially such highly-charged words as these, and make sure that your reader knows exactly what you mean, too.

Words can also have "favorable or unfavorable or neutral meanings, with general or restricted application."[5] Don't use a word with negative connotations unless that's what you want. *Insinuate*, for example, has negative connotations, whereas *suggest* doesn't. Other examples: "*verbiage* connotes a foolish or superfluous display of words and not merely an output of words (*wordage*), good or bad."[6] When you say, "The book reflects on the writer," in this usage "*reflect on* means . . . the same thing as *throw discredit on*."[7] Because of the connotation of words, you can see that the "territory" a word covers "gives access to absurd error on one side and the sharpest precision on the other."[8]

So when you use a word, you must know what it means *and* what it suggests. You must know "its quality" or "atmosphere"[9] as well as its precise meaning.

7. Beware of malapropisms: the mistake of confusing "long words . . . with others that resemble them in sound." "The planned Office of Education Liaison should not *impinge* [infringe] upon the authority of the board." Barzun explains that "this mistake also brought about the false use of *upon* after *infringe*. The sentence should read: 'not infringe the authority of . . . .' "[10] A malapropism can stem from a confusion of the ear or from a confusion in the meanings of closely related words. To avoid these problems, watch carefully for "important distinctions" such as the following: "*repel* and *repulse*; *precipitate* and *precipitous*; *expose*, *exposure* and *exposition*; *assure* and *insure*; *alternative* and *alternate*; *seasonal* and *seasonable*; *heartburn* and *heartburning*; *assignation* and *assignments*; *perspicacious* and *perspicuous*; *diverse* and *divers*; *enormousness* and *enormity*; *relics* and *relicts*; *militate* and *mitigate* . . . ."[11]

8. People don't "blurt" *long* sentences. Use the appropriate verbs and avoid those that have become clichés—such as *gushed* or *chortled*—unless they really serve best for your purpose.[12]

9. Use words with double meanings carefully. For example, *due to* can mean both *because* and also *owing to*. As Kilpatrick shows, *since* and *while* can also cause trouble. If you mean *because* when you use either of these words, Kilpatrick suggests that you use *because* to avoid confusion.[13]

10. Use the simplest, clearest words. In general, this means using short words instead of long ones. But you must take care in following this rule, because to avoid monotony often requires varying word choice. Also, don't sacrifice precision. If the longer word transmits exactly what you want to say, stick with it. Trimble says, "Use the fewest words possible and the simplest words possible. Occasionally . . . the longer word will be the only right word: it may express the idea concisely, or contribute just the rhythm and texture wanted, or gratify your reader with the joy of surprise."[14] Vary your words by using appropriate synonyms. Kubis and Howland advise not to use the same word twice in a paragraph (other than *and*, *the*, and similar words). "Prune out duplicate words," they advise.[15] Don't get stuck in ruts caused by lazy word repetition. But remember that generally simplicity is the goal. Never fool yourself through the use of ornate language: "Oratory should never be asked to substitute for accuracy and truth."[16]

11. Avoid ponderous, pompous language: *not* "human beings cannot possibly apprehend or comprehend the fullness of truth by means of their own finite resources, but can attain it only through the direct intervention of the supernatural Spirit of God," *but*, as Pascal said, "truth . . . is an unattainable quarry, . . . at home in heaven, lying in the lap of God, to be known only in so far as it pleases him to reveal it."[17] Simplify language, but at the same time avoid the drily prosaic, using imaginative metaphor when it fits. The example from Pascal succeeds in this as well. Often the difference between mediocrity and art is a word or two, or a phrase or the turn of a phrase that jump starts a dead writing.

12. "Prefer the short word to the long; the concrete to the abstract; and the familiar to the unfamiliar." But:

> Modify these guidelines in the light of the occasion, the full situation, which includes the likely audience for your words.[18]

13. Avoid "vague words and 'vogue words.' " Examples: "*dimension*, *interface*, *gap* (as in *credibility gap*, *capability gap*, *reality gap*), *realistic*, *processing*, *replicate*, *operational,* and many more, usually Latin derivatives three or four syllables long."[19] Words that end in *-ize* should set your caution light flashing. "Such words or phrases are vague from the start or become so by vogue—over-use."[20] Modern mass culture exudes these words, which become thought-clogging clichés: "*meaningful* dialogue" means what?

14. "Weed out . . . jargon."[21] Example: "Relevant case law deals with the duty of disclosure upon a physician seeking consent to treatment from his patient. Nondisclosure is permitted if it is reasonable when compared to appropriate standards of practice. Of course, such nondisclosure must be premised on harmful effects the information would have." Loose translation: doctors don't have to tell you their treatment will make you sick. Jargon covers truth. For example, the second sentence in this statement, translated out of jargon, means: "A doctor can conceal information from his patient if other doctors would agree that this is okay."

"Look for *all* fancy wordings and get rid of them."[22] Don't use a foreign phrase, a scientific word, a jargon word or a Latin derivative when a good, everyday Anglo-

Saxon English equivalent serves just as well.[23] Say "late nineteenth-century Paris," not "*fin de siècle* Paris"; say "guess," not "hypothesize"; say "choosing who should live and who should die," not "maximize the number of rational creatures whose lives are preserved"; say "jailed," not "incarcerated"; say "worsened" not "exacerbated."

The appeal of jargon "lies in the desire to appear learned and its use also favors laziness. Analyzing ideas is work, especially when the ideas are one's own; and covering up the confusion under phraseology that sounds technical is a quick way out. Once the mind has fallen into this habit, nothing but abstract nouns seems appropriate."[24]

15. Don't mint words unless you can't find an appropriate word that will do the job you need done.[25]

16. Avoid "short, crackling words much too violent for the occasion." Example: Don't say, "The telephone *smashed* the silence of the room," when you mean, "The ring of the telephone *broke* the silence."[26]

17. Use contractions unless inappropriate to the formality of the message conveyed. Generally, replacing *don't* with *do not* and *won't* with *would not* makes your writing sound stilted and overly formal; in some writing, however, the contractions demean the subject discussed.

18. "Avoid archaic words such as: zounds, egad, whence, forsooth, whilst, opined" and so on.[27] Never use *amongst.*

Cut Excess Words

19. Avoid wordiness. Express yourself compactly by cutting needless words. (A needless word is one that can be cut without losing meaning.)

> We all love a man who says a great deal in a few

> words. Most of us feel that life will be too short; so we praise the person who can hammer the nail with only three blows.[28]

Use *suggest* instead of "appears to be suggestive of the possibility that"; use *near* instead of "in close proximity to" and so on.[29]

20. "Prune excess pet words: *as*, *as he*, *so*, *that*, *which*, *this,"* *who, what*—"any word you overuse" and that adds no meaning. For example, in the sentence, "It's the reason that you want to write," cut *that*. "Have someone proof your manuscript and circle excess pet words."[30] Strunk and White call such words "mannerisms."[31] Fight them off!

21. Eliminate words that add no meaning. Watch especially your use of such words as *kind, thing, all*. For example, change "Marvin is the kind of man who likes to eat his salad before his meal" to "Marvin likes to eat salad before meals."

22. Don't be redundant. Don't say, "This happens only occasionally": "This happens occasionally" suffices, because *occasionally* carries the meaning of *only* here. The "*unknown* stranger" or the "*deceitful* liar" are redundant. "He contacted his friend, who received his letter" contains a redundancy: if his friend received the man's letter, then the man has contacted him.

23. Cut any needless material, be it a word, sentence, paragraph, page, section, chapter or whatever.

Clarity and Diction

24. Strive always for clarity and for smoothness; cut out the awkward and the choppy.

25. Don't say anything "that is avoidably ugly."[32]

26. Don't shift "diction level" or "use . . . distracting diction."[33] The following example illustrates these problems: ". . . Her cheeks were thick and smooth and held a healthy natural red color. The heavy lines under them, her jowls, extended to the intersection of her lips and gave her a thick-lipped frown most of the time." Gardner explains that the first phrase—"Her cheeks were thick and smooth"—"is normal English," but then the next phrase, "[Her cheeks] held a healthy natural red color," is written in "elevated, pseudo-poetic" language, mainly through the use of the word *held.* He points to a similar clash in the next sentence: While "the diction level of 'extended to the intersection of her lips' is high and formal," the sentence ends with the colloquial "most of the time." These sentences take the reader up and down on a linguistic roller coaster. Form and content don't match. Avoid "elevated diction," with its "abstract language ('unique smell'), cliché personification ('[the smell] greeted him'), Latinate language where simple Anglo-Saxon would be preferable ('surveyed the area' for 'looked around'), and so forth."[34]

27. But "strong writers bring together oppositions of one kind or another. Kitchen language and elevated language, long and short sentences, fast and slow rhythms. And what they choose to present from life—whether it be object, act, or idea—is frequently the negative and the positive, one thing and its opposite, two ideas that antagonize each other. The result is tension. And the surprise that comes from new combinations. And news."[35] (The apparent clash between this rule and the one above highlights the necessity to apply all these guidelines flexibly, guided by your ear and the purpose of your writing. Both rules are true, but you must decide when each applies.)

Right Verbs and Prepositions

28. Watch for what Barzun calls the "direction" of words. This indicates "the ways that words point when linked with other words." He gives the following example:

> "Every owner was issued with two keys." The very idea of *issuing* is that of *going out*, here of *giving* from hand to hand, so that the mind rebels at the notion of *giving* every owner *with* two keys. The notion of *furnished with* is the deceiving phrase hovering nearby. What then? "Two keys were given to each owner" would be simplest and best . . . .[36]

Generally, words (particularly verbs) can have one of two alternative directions: "transitive," which indicates "*carrying across*," and "intransitive," which means "not" doing so.[37] For example, the following wrongly changes a transitive into an intransitive:

> "The second woman, Mrs. B., is the one with whom they have been fostered for the past 30 months." Mrs. B. was the foster mother; she fostered (that is, fed and cared for) the children; everything in *foster* goes from her to them; they were fostered by her. (emphasis in original)[38]

Therefore they can't "*have been fostered with* her . . . ."[39] Another example of mistakenly transforming a transitive into an intransitive:

> "He never lost his *fascination* for 'The Miller and His Men.' " Ask yourself what *fascinate* means. It means stare at a person or animal (snake versus rabbit) so as to paralyze the victim. In the common law, witchcraft was often called fascination. Figuratively the word has come to mean the . . . power exerted by a work of art as well as a person. It is therefore the tale about the miller that performs the fascination—that "holds" it—and not the man being fascinated; and if that is so, he cannot lose the

> fascination, though the story might. Write: " 'The Miller and His Men' never lost its power to fascinate him"; or "He never ceased being fascinated by . . . ."[40]

Other examples: you can't have "*convictions toward* Communism," but you can have "leanings toward." You can't stroll streets; you stroll along streets. Not "Times Square is *purported to be* the crossroads of the world" but "purports to be."[41] Remembering the distinction between transitive and intransitive will help you to not mix up those commonly confused words: "*sit* and *set*, *lie* and *lay*, *rise* and *raise*." In each pair, the first is intransitive and the second transitive. So, "you sit" but "you set it down," "you lie" but "you lay it down," "you rise" but "you raise it up."

Another confusion that this distinction between intransitive and transitive will enable us to avoid: "We are ecology-minded. This bag will *self-destruct* in mother earth." This second sentence is false, since the bag won't destroy itself in the earth but will "be destroyed" by the action of the elements upon it. Furthermore, there is no verb *destruct*: the proper word is *destroy*. "In case of rapture, this car will self-destruct" is impossible diction, because

> *it will self-destruct* cannot mean *it will destroy itself*, because a transitive requires a direct object to complete its meaning. You do not say *my car will self-start, stunt fliers often self-kill*, and the like. Direction in words is all-important in that it commands the presence or absence of other words.[42]

29. Use the appropriate *prepositions*. "Certain verbs take one preposition invariably, others several with different meanings, still others take none. Respect each type of link."[43] Prepositions link the verb to what the verb does, and so a wrong preposition can throw everything off balance.

These "stocky, independent little words" (prepositions) are "full of purpose and self-assurance" and without "deceit," "hidden dangers" or "nonsense." They usually "form a lever between a verb and a noun" and "give a particular focus to a verb." "They qualify," but without weakening.[44]

They can sometimes give two distinct motions to one verb: "The gull flew *out from* and *down* the cliff."[45]

They can sometimes act so powerfully that we don't even need the verb: "Out brief candle!"[46]

Barzun explains that usually "the wanted preposition goes with the one buried in the word: *con-* (*com-*) means *with* and calls for *with*."[47] Example: "Major André's arrest revealed Benedict Arnold's treasonous *com*munication *with* the British."

Another rule:

> . . . When you use two verbs in a row with a single object following, either both verbs must take the same preposition or the first must take none . . . . : "His experience makes him the best person to *tackle* and succeed *in* his difficult task." (emphasis in original)[48]

Don't give prepositions to verbs that take none, such as *consider*, *infringe*, and *commiserate*. People fall into this because they confuse the verbs with other words, usually their synonyms. For example, "*Infringe* (your rights) suggests *encroach* (upon) and out comes *infringe upon*. *Consider* suggests *regard*, which needs *as*. If you are tempted to say, 'I consider you as a fool,' remember that you are applying the epithet to yourself."[49]

Remember the direction of your words, and you'll use the proper preposition:

> Consider *delineate*. Its bare meaning is *draw a line*, but connotation dictates that the line drawn be *around* an object or situation to depict it, not

> *between* two entities to separate them. Hence the request heard in a Massachusetts court: "Can you *delineate between* the checks you deposited at your bank and those you kept at your firm?" violates both the connotation and the direction of the verb.[50]

One verb can take different prepositions depending upon its direction. You *agree with* "a person or point of view" but *agree to* "a set of conditions and *upon* a plan of action."[51]

> Any writer can *compare himself with* Shakespeare and discover how far he falls short; if he *compares himself to* Shakespeare (that is, puts himself on the same level), then he had better think again. Under the law everybody is *subject to* punishment, but only a small number are *subjected* to it.[52]

30. Replace passive verbs with action verbs. Use strong verbs: "a strong verb is a common word used in an uncommon place." Weak: "The woman sat thinking about how to get revenge on her husband." Strong: "The woman sat embroidering revenge."[53] But avoid overwriting and clichés (both discussed below).

31. Avoid "linking verbs," which "invite generalization and distance."[54] Whereas active verbs show actions (*walked, jumped, ran, spoke*), linking verbs connect a noun and a word that expresses the condition of the noun: "the mother *seemed* tired." "To be," the most common of these, is discussed in the section on verbs in chapter 4 of *Right Words*. Others include "to feel, to seem, to look, to appear, to experience, to express, to show, to demonstrate, to convey, to display." These words all have important and necessary uses, but they all suggest "that the character is being acted upon or observed by someone rather than doing something."[55] When we say, "He looked happy" or "She demonstrated her impatience," we do not show the reader but we tell him and leave him to guess what the happiness or impatience looked like. Burroway notes that most of these linking verbs have active forms; for example, "the case displayed the fossils" presents an active form, whereas "he displayed his anger" substitutes a *secondhand telling* for a *firsthand*, seeable picture of what this anger looks like. Instead of telling us that the character "displayed his anger" or "became angry," *show* his anger through action, dialogue, description, metaphor, his thoughts or some combination of these. Words such as *display* serve as "linking verbs" when "the only action implied is that of the observer who perceives" the action.[56] But remember also that "linking verbs, like the passive voice, can appropriately convey a sense of passivity or helplessness when that is the desired effect."[57]

32. "Had had's" are "no no's" if at all avoidable. Make that first *had* a contraction if you must use it: "He'd had."[58]

33. " . . . 'As if' takes 'were,' not 'was.' "[59]

34. "Avoid overuse of gerunds, words ending in 'ing.' "[60]

Introductory phrases beginning with *-ing* words "are so common in bad writing that one is wise to treat them as guilty until proven innocent."[61] Such phrases tend to confuse the focus of the sentence or can even lead to "plain illogic." For example, they can make sequential actions seem to occur simultaneously: "Firing the hired man and burning down his shack, Eloise drove into town."[62] Or they can portray impossibilities or at least incongruous situations: "Quickly turning from the bulkhead, Captain Figg spoke slowly and carefully."[63] While it's not impossible that Captain Figg spoke slowly and carefully after turning "quickly . . . from the bulkhead," it would certainly be difficult and strange for him to do so. If he turned quickly, he'd also want to speak quickly. The structure of the sentence here makes Captain Figg's actions seem absurd. But even if such problems don't arise, "too frequent or inappropriate use" of this form "makes bad writing."[64] Even if no confusion results, this type of writing tends to become a boring mannerism. While appropriate at times, use it sparingly; in its place it can "be an excellent thing," as when it "momentarily slows down the action," giving "it a considered, weighted quality that can heighten the tension of an important scene":[65] "Carefully unwrapping the plain brown wrapper, she found a small wooden box." But indiscriminate use "chops the action into fits and starts and loses what effectiveness it might have had, properly set."[66]

Kilpatrick (following Douglas Southall Freeman) also advises against ending sentences with participle phrases. "Beware such sentences as, 'The Mayor refused to discuss the subject, *saying* it was one for consideration of the Council.' "[67] The ending is weak and vague. Better: "Because he saw it as a matter for consideration of the Council, the Mayor refused to discuss the subject."

35. Use *must* rather than *have to* when these expressions are interchangeable.

36. Keep verb tense consistent: don't shift from present to past to present. Again, if you do need to make a shift, give an appropriate signal and then stick consistently with your new verb tense. For example, in the following quote from *The Wild Birds,* Wendell Berry signals the change from present to past first by bringing us back, at the beginning of the second paragraph, to "seventy-five years ago." When in the next sentence Berry writes, "Mat remembers," we have shifted completely to the past. The transition comes smooth and clear, and the reader is left in no doubt about the shift in time frames.

He reaches the edge of the stream at a point

> where the boundary, coming down the slope facing him, turns at a right angle and follows Shade Branch in its fall toward the creek known as Willow Run. Here the fence that Mat has been following crosses the branch over the top of a rock wall that was built in the notch of the stream long before Mat was born. The water coming down, slowed by the wall, has filled the notch above it with rock and silt, and then, in freshet, leaping over it, has scooped out a shallow pool below it, where water stands most of the year. All this, given the continuous little changes of growth and wear in the woods and the stream, is as it was when Mat first knew it: the wall gray and mossy, the water, only a spout now, pouring over the wall into the little pool, covering the face of it with concentric wrinkles sliding outward.
>
> Here, seventy-five years ago, Mat came with a fencing crew: his father, Ben, his uncle, Jack Beechum, Joe Banion, a boy then, not much older than Mat, and Joe's grandfather, Smoke, who had been a slave. And Mat remembers Jack Beechum coming down through the woods, as Mat himself has just come, carrying on his shoulder two of the long light rams they use to tamp the dirt into postholes. As he approached the pool he took a ram in each hand, holding them high, made three long approaching strides, planted the rams in the middle of the pool, and vaulted over. Mat, delighted, said, "Do it again!" And without breaking rhythm, Jack turned, made the three swinging strides, and did it again—*does* it again in Mat's memory, so clearly that Mat's presence there, so long after, fades away, and he hears their old laughter, and hears Joe Banion say, "Mistah Jack, he might nigh a *bird*!"[68]

You might tell your story beginning in the present tense and then switch to the past tense, as Berry does here. But note the smooth way Berry shifts verb tenses to bring the reader back and forth in time between the present and Mat's memories of the past. As Berry does in the above selection, always make clear why you shift verb tenses and then stick consistently with the verb tense you choose until you have some good reason to switch. Here's another example:

> Though tractors draw them now, not horses and mules, there is something in the sound of the wagons going out that is the same as always. Now there is the alien commotion of iron and fire, but within it or under it there is the old rattling and pounding of the empty wagon beds against the bolsters, hurrying out over the rough farm roads in the cool of the morning. As he listened there passed and passed again across the gaze of his memory a team of good mare mules that he bought as three-year-olds from Graham Foresee in the September of 1888.
>
> They were a team of black, mealy-nosed mare mules with plenty of size and depth of body, with a lot of lift in their motion, matched well every way. Beck and Kate. As though the reins are in his hands, and he stands again on the rattling wagon, they are carrying him to the field. The sun is just coming up. It is the fall of the year. The mules are in good flesh, the hair glossy on them, and they are fresh from the night. They step together in the harness with an eager lightness that for a moment shortens his breath.[69]

Clearly the shift takes place as the story changes from "now" to "1888." When we stay in the now, we stay in the present tense; when we move to 1888, we go to the past tense.

In general, for narrative, prefer the past tense. This form, used so universally as to be generally "invisible," will almost always serve the reader best.[70] At times, however, you can "effectively" employ "the present tense . . .

to depict moments of special intensity . . . ." But save the present tense "for those crucial moments" and control it "so carefully in the transition that the reader is primarily aware of the intensity, rather than the tense."[71]

37. While generally to be avoided because its static form generally encourages "abstract, less vital" writing, *it is* can serve as an emphasizer in its proper place, which slows the reader down to make him spend more time on the point.[72]

Right Modifiers

38. "Keep . . . adjectives to a minimum."[73]

39. "Avoid weak (trite) adverbs like *very*, *extremely*, *really* and *terribly*."[74] "*Very* is the least *very* word in the language." Frequently adverbs emphasizing "suddenness—*extremely*, *rapidly*, *suddenly*, *phenomenally*, *quickly*, *immediately*, *instantly*, *definitely*, *terribly*, *awfully*—slow the sentence down" and so "dilute the force of the intended meaning."[75] For example, " 'They stopped very abruptly' is not as abrupt as 'They stopped.' "[76]

40. Don't overload with modifiers that clutter the reader's mind and eye.

41. "Avoid adjective pairs. Example: It was a dark, stormy night; the wind was cold, damp; the eerie, green moon glowed iridescent and ominous. Vary the number of your adjectives in your sentences."[77]

Metaphors and Imagery

42. Use images, metaphors, similes, analogies, idioms, figures of speech and so on to make your meaning clearer and more visible. These should never distract from your meaning but always make that meaning clearer. To do this, they must be "fresh enough to have an effect."[78]

43. Don't use any "metaphor, simile or other figure of speech" that has become a thoughtless cliché through overuse.[79]

44. Don't mix your metaphors. Metaphors serve as aids to seeing. If you put together metaphors that pull in different directions, you confuse your reader and obstruct his vision. Examples: "The fascist octopus has sung its swan song." "The jackboot is thrown into the melting pot . . . ."[80]

45. "Consult your second thoughts about slang, euphemisms, and 'what everybody says,' so as to make your diction entirely your own choice."[81] Even if people commonly say that "bloodshed flared," does it make sense to say it?

Showing and Details

46. Give sufficient detail to enable the reader to see what you want to show him. Remember to address *all* five senses as much as possible.

47. Eliminate "unnecessary abstraction." Use the concrete and specific word, not the abstract. Use it actively, not passively. Abstract writing "is a by-product of scientific writing. In trying to remain impersonal and detached, it becomes flabby and obscure, because the lack of agents and of strong verbs deprives the sentence of its due motive power and needed signposts."[82] Look at the following example:

> If enforcible deprivations are provided for deviational conduct, the mature members of the community are expected to take these possible deprivations into account as potential costs in assessing the balance of indulgence and deprivation attendant upon behavioral alternatives.[83]

Barzun translates these almost impenetrable abstractions to mean:

> Knowing that the law punishes crime, mature people will weigh the risks and think twice before they do wrong.[84]

As Barzun notes, this writer probably avoids such words as "crime and wrong" deliberately, because he wants to foster a morally neutral view.[85] So he erases any morally responsible human beings committing crimes against other human beings and replaces people with the abstraction of "deviational conduct." Similarly, he wipes away the image of jail cells and electric chairs and replaces them with the abstraction of "enforcible deprivations."

Such use of abstractions, Barzun warns, destroys "the power of thinking in both reader and writer, so that neither can test for himself the truth or falsity of what is said." No one can test the thought because no one can see it. It disappears in the fog of abstraction. Instead of presenting such abstractions, you should "grasp . . . an 'imageable' subject and then tell us what it does or has done to another of a like kind."[86] Show criminals stealing property and beating people, rather than speaking of "deviational conduct." Show criminals locked in jail instead of speaking of "enforcible deprivations." Avoid as much as possible words that end in *-tion* or *-ment.*

48. Give specific descriptions. Don't say "wonderful day," but show in visual language what kind of day you mean. Banal generalizations show nothing to the reader.

49. Lace your writing, especially necessary abstractions, with examples, "graphic illustrations, analogies, apt quotations, and concrete details."[87]

50. Avoid explainery.[88] Show rather than tell. (See point 31 above.)

Names

51. Never miss "the chance to call a thing by its *proper* name." A name provides a "most available device for being particular, for defining exactly" your "authority," "for defining exactly" your "love."[89]

In the following passage, the use of plant names helps the reader to see and so gives confidence in the reliability of the writer:

> The two windows in the back wall look out in a narrow lot covered with dead weed stalks, chicory and poke and burdock, and the lighter brown napping of foxtail and wild oat.[90]

Look at the difference between these two passages:

> Several days later the Governor came with his wife, who was a Jewess. He sent for the prisoner and listened to him as he spoke about faith in God. As the prisoner discoursed on righteousness, self-control and the judgment to come, the Governor was afraid and said, "That's enough for now! You may leave. When I find it convenient, I will send for you." At the same time he was hoping that the prisoner would offer him a bribe, so he sent for him frequently and talked with him.

> Several days later Felix came with his wife Drusilla, who was a Jewess. He sent for Paul and listened to him as he spoke about faith in Christ Jesus. As Paul discoursed on righteousness, self-control and the judgment to come, Felix was afraid and said, "That's enough for now! You may leave. When I find it convenient, I will send for you." At the same time he was hoping that Paul would offer him a bribe, so he sent for him frequently and talked with him. (Acts 24:24-26)

Macrorie says:

> When you have to mention anything in order to tell a story or make a point, force yourself to put down the name of that thing if it has a name, or to show it in its particular setting or doing its thing particularly. Don't say you pushed the throttle and the motorbike did its thing. Give the name of that thing and the sound and feel or smell, or whatever you can.[91]

52. Name dropping of boulevards, streets, parks and so on, however, can't substitute for focused, telling description of those places that put the reader there. When you write about real places, also remember that you commit yourself to following real layout. If in a fictional story you plan to change geography, you need to make your reader understand why you've done so. For example, one writer wanted to change some place settings in New Orleans, so he warned his readers at the onset of his book that while he wrote about "New Orleans," he had made it into a fictional place that didn't conform exactly to the geography of the city of that name.

The Sound of Words

53. Eliminate accidental rhymes unless it fits your purpose.[92]

54. To see if your sentences flow and have impact and rhythm, read your writing aloud. (See rule 4.) When you read out loud, you hear the words in your mind at the same time that you see them on the page. When the writer reads his words out loud, it helps him know what the reader will hear in his mind. This helps the writer to listen for the *cadence*, the *rhythm*, the sound of his words. Watch for *alliteration* (repetition of an initial sound), *assonance* (a correspondence of sound between words and syllables), *rhyme*,[93] *onomatopoeia* ("words whose sounds imitate or echo the sound they describe"[94]) and so on. When used effectively, these are all very powerful devices. When used poorly, they ruin otherwise effective writing.

Fairfax and Moat look into the assonance in these lines from Shakespeare:

> Aye, but to die, and go we know not where,
> To lie in cold obstruction, and to rot;
> This sensible warm motion to become
> A kneaded clod; and the delighted spirit
> To bathe in fiery floods; or to reside
> In thrilling regions of thick-ribbed ice.[95]

Their comment on the sounds and rhythms:

> There are two main themes, the "i" theme and the "o" theme. Read it aloud and listen how they play against each other. A thing that is beautiful is the way the "i" theme is established at the beginning in "staccato" of pure rhyme; then later it is reintroduced, but now muted in mere assonance (delight, reside, ice) to ring like an echo. Listen also for the minor theme of the e's in lines 1, 4 and 6. But finally what is wonderful is that when one reads great writing each sound is *telling* and seems set absolutely true. True to the mood, the drama, and the tune.[96]

What potential lurks in all these simply given words!

55. Cut out weak repetitions, but "remember that strong

repetition is the heart of all good writing, in fact the heart of all good music making, hurdle racing, hammering, walking . . . . Repetitions set up pattern. Only with pattern can you achieve emphasis and variety. Da-da-da, da-da-da, da-da-dum. That *dum* is smart because it comes after all those *da's*. It picks up its power as you wait through all those *da's* for something to happen. Repeat and vary. That's the secret of achieving significant form in all art and communication." But weak repetitions "get in the readers' way rather than drive them down your road."[97]

Sentence Structure

56. Anytime someone must read a sentence twice because of form (not content), recast the sentence.

57. "Never use the passive where you can use the active," unless the passive expresses your meaning more clearly or more powerfully. Don't use the passive without good reason. Generally the good reason is the need for the passive form to give emphasis to some point. The following gives some examples.[98]

"Choose the passive . . . because you want to put its subject first in the sentence or because you do not know, or do not want to reveal, who is performing the action."[99] Strunk and White point out that "the need of making a particular word the subject of the sentence will often . . . determine which voice is to be used."[100]

Williams explains one way to determine when the passive is appropriate:

> The problem—and the challenge—of English prose is that in almost every sentence we write, we have to strike the best compromise among the principles of clarity and directness . . . , the

> emphasis we intend, and those principles of coherence and cohesion that fuse separate sentences into a whole discourse. *But in that compromise, we must always give priority to emphasis and cohesion, to what fuses sentences into cohesive discourse.* (emphasis in original)[101]

In other words, sentences don't stand on their own; they must link up with other sentences. The structure of the sentence is largely determined by its relationship to other sentences. He gives the following example in which a passive construction works better than the active. First, he looks at a particular sentence to see how it works best when standing on its own:

> A black hole is created by the collapse of a dead star into a point perhaps no larger than a marble.
>
> The collapse of a dead star into a point perhaps no larger than a marble creates a black hole.[102]

By itself, the second, active, structure is better. But then Williams places the sentence in this context, the ellipses standing for the place where the above-quoted sentence would go:

> Some astonishing questions about the nature of the universe have been raised by scientists exploring the nature of black holes in space . . . . So much matter compressed into so little volume changes the fabric of space around it in profoundly astonishing ways.[103]

Here the thought would flow more smoothly if the passive form were used for the missing sentence, linking the concept *black holes* at the end of the first sentence with *black hole* at the beginning of the second. Williams remarks that "our sense of coherence and rhythm should tell us" the need for the passive voice here.[104] In other words, don't try to think it all out—simply give yourself to the given rhythm of relationships.

Yet for clarification he presents the following general rules:

> *Whenever possible, express at the beginning of a sentence ideas already stated, referred to, implied, safely assumed, familiar, predictable, less important, readily accessible information.*[105]
>
> *Express at the end of a sentence the least predictable, the newest, the most important, the most significant information, the information you almost certainly want to emphasize.*[106]

The passive, then, can help rearrange sentences to improve cohesion and emphasis. To illustrate, Williams gives another example of the proper use of the passive, to "switch a long subject full of new information for a short one that repeats something already mentioned or relatively more familiar."[107] The example:

> During the first years of our Republic, *a series of brilliant and virtuous presidents committed to a democracy yet confident in their own special competence* conducted **its administration**.
> During the first years of our Republic, **its administration** was conducted *by a series of brilliant and virtuous presidents committed to a democracy, yet confident in their own special competence.*[108]

This represents only a guide. Again, your own voice and sense of rhythm will guide you naturally if you'll listen.

58. "Sentences should not be so long that the reader loses his way in them."[109]

> We must either stick close to the simple [sentence] structures we have learned to manage orally, or we must learn to pay attention more carefully to what we are doing when we generate an extended or complicated sentence. If, for example, we drift into a long sentence, full of items that interrupt the flow, some of which are relative clauses which have within them other

relative clauses and parenthetical remarks—like this one—that distract our attention from the fact that we began with an "if" which requires a "then" before the structure can be completed, then we must not forget how we have started or abandon our structure in the middle from confusion, forgetting that a sentence with an "if" and a "then" may well need a "but" before it can complete itself comfortably, but we must persevere, concentrating intently, holding the thought in our head and our breath in our lungs, while we race furiously toward that blissful moment when we can conclude with that perfect and appropriate mark of punctuation: the period. There. Was it worth it? Sometimes it is. Sometimes the complexity of our thought can be accommodated only in a complex sentence, but often it is neither necessary nor desirable. Every deviation from simplicity and directness must be justified in two ways: first by your ability to sustain your grammar over the long haul, and second by the necessity for a complex sentence at that moment in your thinking.[110]

59. Vary sentences in length and structure.[111] Avoid monotony, but take care not to embrace novelty for its own sake. "Seek to leave the meaning of the sentence incomplete until the last word. Add nothing after the meaning is complete. Start a new sentence then."[112] So avoid "that" or "which" clauses that detract from the central action of the sentence[113]: "When she walked out of the room, he quickly grabbed the bulging envelope from the open drawer which lay on the right side of the wooden desk." Such sentences "trail off," losing energy[114] and distracting the reader from the story rather than bringing him more deeply into it.

60. Give each sentence a clear focus, enabling the reader to see a clear image.[115]

61. Use rhythm properly.[116] Recognize that your choice of words and structure gives your sentences a rhythm: short and choppy, slow and languid, and so on. Again, try to make form and content agree.

In the first example, short, fast sentences portray a battle between an old man and sharks that try to devour the great fish he has caught and strapped to his boat:

> The other shark had been in and out and now came in again with his jaws wide. The old man could see pieces of the meat of the fish spilling white from the corner of his jaws as he bumped the fish and closed his jaws. He swung at him and hit only the head and the shark looked at him and wrenched the meat loose. The old man swung the club down on him again as he slipped away to swallow and hit only the heavy solid rubberiness.
>
> "Come on, *galano*," the old man said. "Come in again."
>
> The shark came in a rush and the old man hit him as he shut his jaws. He hit him solidly and from as high up as he could raise the club.[117]

The second example contains long, leisurely sentences portraying a banquet table in middle-class Dublin:

> A fat brown goose lay at one end of the table and at the other end, on a bed of creased paper strewn with sprigs of parsley, lay a great ham, stripped of its outer skin and peppered over with crust crumbs, a neat paper frill round its shin and beside this was a round of spiced beef. Between these rival ends ran parallel lines of side-dishes: two little minsters of jelly, red and yellow; a shallow dish full of blocks of blancmange and red jam, a large green leaf-shaped dish with a stalk-shaped handle, on which lay bunches of purple raisins and peeled almonds, a companion dish on which lay a solid rectangle of Smyrna figs, a dish of custard topped with grated nutmeg, a small bowl full of chocolates and sweets wrapped in gold and silver papers and a glass vase in which stood some tall celery stalks.[118]

62. In a sentence where "several nouns, phrases or clauses depend on the same verb, put the longer phrase or clause *last*." So don't write: "He addressed the General Assembly, the members of the Corporation Commission and the Governor."[119]

63. "In conditional sentences, seek to put the conditional clause *before* the principal clause. An *if* clause at the beginning of a sentence is better placed than at the end, unless the whole point of the sentence lies in the *if*."[120]

Not:

We must understand the European culture the American colonists fled if we want to understand them.

Instead:

If we want to understand the American colonists, we must first understand the European culture they fled.

But:

You can certainly achieve your goal, if you're willing to pay the price.

64. "Make every antecedent plain: Never permit 'it' or 'that' or any similar word to refer to different things in the same sentence."[121] Example: "The plane fell rapidly toward the craggy mountain peak, high above the tree line. It seemed to jump up to meet it as the plane plummeted out of control." Either the first or second *it* needs identifying to eliminate all confusion.

65. Don't use "this" when the reader won't know what "this" is. Always be specific. "Always ask yourself what you mean when you want to use the word 'this.' If you don't know, neither will the reader." Example: "Any story more than a few pages will fail unless it sets up and satisfies the reader's plot expectations. This must be the writer's greatest concern." Specify what "this" is. In this case, the writer probably means "plotting."

66. While not intrinsically wrong, some writing devices have become clichéd through overuse. For example, the use of *as* and *while* in the following sentences exemplifies a method that writers have used repeatedly over the years to pack more information into their sentences:

> "No," he said, *as* he leaned back in his chair.
>
> "What's up with you?" asked Mary, *while* raising her can of Diet Coke.[122]

When you write such sentences, try when possible to find some other way to include this information:

> He leaned back in his chair. "No," he said.
>
> Mary raised her can of Diet Coke. "What's up with you?" she asked.

67. Don't fall into "mannerism,"[123] the overuse of a word, phrase or technique of writing. A word used well once or twice becomes a mannerism by unthinking, habitual repetition. It then begins to bore and even irritate the reader. The habitual (as opposed to purposeful—see point 55) repetition of *any* word, phrase or literary device becomes a distracting, annoying mannerism. (Employ synonym finders and thesauruses in your war against this vice.)

Examples: Continually repeating the same form when introducing quotes from various authors: "*As* Kittel points out . . . . *As* Jacques Ellul remarks . . . . *As* Van Til says . . . ."

Repeatedly using the same form as a transition from one section to the next: "*Let us* begin by showing . . . . *Let us* now demonstrate . . . . *Let us* examine . . . . *Let us* look at this problem . . . ."

Regularly using the same word over and over for emphasis: "*Actually* the attempts of the government to assist the farmer have *actually* had the effect of shifting his dependence from the market to the compulsory power of the government . . . ."

68. Remember that "the most emphatic place in clause or sentence is the end. This is the climax . . . the last word. One should therefore think twice about what one puts at a sentence-end."[124]

This is true not only of sentences but also paragraphs, chapters, essays and books. To get somewhere, you must know your destination. So many writers begin by writing their ending. The ending is "constructed of information that matters to the reader."[125] The ending should "leave some room for the reader." Rather than telling him "how to think or feel," we should "deliver information that will" permit the reader to think and feel the truth for himself. "The ending works or it doesn't work. Nothing you can say will make weak information strong. Deliver a solid piece of information—and stop."[126]

69. Whenever possible, use the positive form rather than the negative. (I wrote this instead of "Don't use the negative form, but rather use the positive form if not impossible.") Readers, Strunk and White insist, want to know what is, and "consciously or unconsciously" feel "dissatisfied with being told only what is not."[127]

70. Avoid exaggerating and equivocating. Statements should not be made more forceful or more doubtful than they are. Use *obviously*, *of course*, *clearly*, *certainly*, *surely* and similar terms only when something really will be apparent and certain to the reader (which is not so often as we would like to believe). Save words that express uncertainty—"*would, should, could, may, might,* and *can*"[128]—for genuine ambiguities.

Eliminate False Voice

71. Eliminate everything "awkward, phony, or forced."[129]

72. Eliminate sentimentality, "the attempt to get some effect without providing due cause." In contrast to *sentiment*, which means feeling and emotion, and which is indispensable for powerful writing, particularly narrative, *sentimentality* indicates "emotion or feeling that rings false, usually because achieved by some form of cheating or exaggeration."[130] The reader sees emotion as true only when it results from "drama; that is, character in action."[131] The reader wants to *experience* actions that evoke emotions; he doesn't want cue cards announcing what he should feel. Avoid sentimentality by showing rather than telling and by presenting appropriate metaphors. This doesn't mean to avoid strong feelings when appropriate. Failure to portray appropriate feelings evidences "frigidity."[132] This "occurs" when the writer "reveals by some slip or self-regarding intrusion" less concern for "his characters than" he ought to feel.[133] In tone, image or in some other way, he does not respond appropriately to the situation of his characters. A "real writer" possesses a "nobility of spirit" that enables him to "enter deeply into the feelings" of his "characters (as he enters deeply into the feelings of real people)."[134] Frigidity is the antipode of sentimentality, and both problems are corrected by matching form and content.

Frigidity marks a "writer who presents serious material" but then refuses to follow through "with the attention and seriousness" the subject deserves. Because he coldly refuses to open his heart to care about, to feel, to express the depth of emotion the subject warrants, he treats something deep and tender as profane. The frigid writer is unable "to recognize the seriousness of things in the first place." He refuses to face "real feeling," to allow himself to experience deep emotion, and sees only the surface of human conflicts.[135] Frigidity marks an increasing trend in writing, exalting empty form above content, character and meaning. Frigidity may show itself as the effort to force emotion and hence can cause its seeming opposite, sentimentality. It also lies behind a writer's willingness to let inferior work stand even when he himself recognizes its inferiority. "When a skillful writer writes a shallow, cynical, merely amusing book about extramarital affairs, he has wandered—with far more harmful effect—into the same unsavory bog."[136] He shows that he is a person for whom normal feelings have been replaced by a laugh.

73. Avoid melodrama. Whereas drama convincingly and subtly brings "out the importance of seemingly small things," melodrama shows "large things grappling and clashing."[137] Rather than focusing on the "ordinary" and the readily credible, melodrama concentrates on the "remarkable," that which lies at "the ends of the spectrum" of "reality."[138] But, again, because melodrama "ignores" the "ordinary" to concentrate on the "unusual and unlikely," it has a "credibility problem."[139] Its villains are too fully evil and its heroes too fully good to be believable: the bad guy twirling his mustache and laughing hysterically, the good guy standing erect with polished forehead and every hair always perfectly in place. Melodrama tends toward one-dimensionality and eliminates the inner conflicts within each person. It is shallow and superficial, a thin stone skipping over the surface, never immersed but flying from one bank to another. Of course, we must sometimes deal with "large things . . . clashing," "the ends of the spectrum" and the "extraordinary." Yet when we do so, we must heighten realism and the depth of our exploration of character, carefully avoiding oversimplifications. Such deep psychological character studies can usually only be carried and sustained by "large things grappling." So melodrama isn't just the clash of the remarkable but also avoids any depth and showing with "little regard for convincing motivation." Instead, it offers "an excessive appeal to the emotions of the audience." The melodrama seeks merely to arouse "strong feelings of pity or horror or joy" disproportionate to the true dramatic context of the story.[140] It thus tends toward manipulative devices, for example, showing a child threatened by death or great physical harm, but without any truthful explanation of why the danger comes.

Melodrama thus frequently serves as a propaganda device, warning of dangers out of all proportion to the actual situation in order to justify unjustifiable "preventative" measures. An example of melodrama in the service of propaganda is the Russian Communist film *Potemkin* by Sergei Eisenstein, where Czarist cruelty and Bolshevik heroism are both ludicrously exaggerated. In this film about a Bolshevik-led mutiny aboard a Czarist battleship in 1905, the Czarist officers walk with perpetual sneers on their faces, delighting in the suffering of the sailors. The Bolsheviks, in contrast, absolutely brim with compassion, nobility, honesty. No depth of character nor internal conflicts mar the Marxist oversimplification. So don't produce similar "Christian" oversimplifications that distort reality in this same way. Rather make your writing express the depth of inner conflicts that shape real human beings.

74. Eliminate "mannered writing,"*

> . . . writing that continually distracts us from the [narrative] by stylistic tics that we cannot help associating, as we read, with the author's wish

* This is different from "mannerism" spoken of in point 67.

> to intrude himself, prove himself different from all other authors.[141]

Gardner remarks that

> the tics of mannered writing . . . are those from which we gather, by the prickling of our thumbs, some ulterior purpose on the writer's part, a purpose perhaps not fully conscious but nevertheless suspect, putting us on our guard . . . . Whereas the frigid writer lacks strong feeling, and the sentimental writer applies feeling indiscriminately, the mannered writer feels more strongly about his own personality and ideas—his ego, which he therefore keeps before us by means of style—than he feels about any of his characters—in effect, all the rest of humanity.[142]

Gardner mentions the example of the pontifications of the socialist playwright George Bernard Shaw. Alexander Cockburn, a socialist journalist, offers a more contemporary sample of such "mannered writing" in his account of his return to a boarding school he had attended as a young boy:

> But now it was October, the track was bare and the enclosure empty. My taxi driver said that he had heard that Heatherdown was to be sold for real-estate development once the film crew had gone. The driveway, fringed with *fateful* rhododendrons, looked much the same and *at last* I entered the front door. Heatherdown had actually been built as a school just before the First World War, unlike many of the prep schools round about which were simply converted Victorian country houses with maids' rooms converted into diminutive dormitories. All such schools were divided into the boys' zone of activity—classrooms, dormitories and the like—and the headmaster's private quarters. The room of concern to us was the headmaster's study, thickly carpeted, *fragrant with tobacco and terror*. It was here that we were

> summoned for *interrogation* and punishment. In *exact evocation* of Freud's essay on *Haemlichkeit*—"homeliness" with *a sinister and uncanny core*—the study was both the closest echo of distant home and a parent's love but also *the Colosseum for the unleashed superego.* My own father never beat me. The closest he ever got to it was saying once that had any other father endured such injury (I had let down the tires of his bicycle to stop him from going into town one evening), this other father would have thrashed his son savagely. But here, hundreds of miles from the security of my own father's study, was this *ersatz* study, inhabited by the father-substitute who did indeed—on a few occasions—beat me with a clothes brush, once for repeatedly trying to conceal from Matron the fact that I had again wet my bed. (emphasis added)[143]

This writing is preposterous. Yet its absurdity flows not from lack of intelligence but from the writer's pampered obsession with himself and the sound of his own voice. We have italicized some of the more mannered touches, beginning with his plunge into the pathetic fallacy: in what sense are the rhododendrons "fateful"? Then, he tells us that "at last" he "entered the front door," as though some great throng waited expectantly for his grand entrance. The headmaster's room is "fragrant with tobacco and terror"; it served as "the Colosseum for the unleashed superego." "Colosseum" evokes the insidious tortures inflicted upon the victims of the Caesars, as when naked men and women were strapped to red hot iron chairs. What was this terror, this torture, that awaited Cockburn here: the headmaster had "indeed—on a few occasions" beat him "with a clothes brush." This chamber of horrors brought forth for Cockburn an "exact evocation" of the image of "homeliness" masking "a sinister and uncanny core"; beneath the headmaster's benign grin lurked the ultimate pain and insult humanly bearable—a paddling with a clothes brush. This room was an "ersatz study," Cockburn tells us. *Ersatz* can mean "substitute," but it brings forth the image of the contrived and false. *Webster's New World Dictionary*, explaining that "the word usually suggests inferior quality," gives as one of its meanings *synthetic* and offers as a synonym *artificial*.[144] In what sense, then, was the headmaster's study "ersatz"? Again, only from Cockburn's petulant infantile perspective. Yet in this paragraph, Cockburn doesn't joke about the way young schoolboys perceived this room; he presents his own adult judgment, now framed in the ideological garb of Freudianism. This coddled ideology forms an example of mannered prose that certainly suggests to us "some ulterior purpose on the writer's part . . ." and the sense that this "writer feels more strongly about his own personality and ideas" than he does about the people and place he writes to or about.

75. Don't overwrite. Again, match form and content. If form envelops and smothers content, whether with excess adjectives, sentimental words, or whatever, then cut and pare.

Continuity and Conjunctions

76. Check for continuity. Every sentence and paragraph should be "manifestly connected to the ones immediately preceding and following it." Your prose should "flow" and "this is the only way to achieve that . . . effect."[145] The better your writing, "the less need . . . for mechanical means of connecting . . . ideas, too many of which tend to clutter an argument." For example, don't keep telling the reader: "Now that we have proven such and such, we shall now go on to prove so and so . . ." or "From point such and such and point so and so, we can conclude . . . ." Rely "chiefly on a coherent understanding of what [you want] to say, a simple style, the occasional repetition of key words, and the careful [*very careful*] use of pronouns such as *this* and *that*."[146]

77. Take care to use exact words to show the sort of continuity that one thought or sentence bears to another. Do you want to contrast one point to another or to show their similarity? Does the sentence expound further on a previous point or does it raise a new one? The appropriate word lets the reader know what to expect. If you send him the wrong signal, you confuse him; he may even suspect you of deliberately misleading him, which could stop him from reading any further and cause him to dismiss what you've already said. Below you will find the key words that help form transitions (in parentheses are less formal equivalents):

above all	in particular
accordingly (and so)	instead
admittedly	in summary
again	likewise (and)
also	moreover
besides	more
specifically (for example)	
but	nevertheless
(but)	
certainly	nonetheless
consequently (and so)	on the other hand
finally	rather
(however, instead)	
first	second
for example	similarly
for instance	so
furthermore	still

hence (therefore)	then
however	therefore
in addition (besides, also)	though
in conclusion (therefore, so)	thus
indeed (in fact)	to sum up
in fact	yet

These words "give your reader the directional signals he needs," since they tell him "how your ideas connect."[147]

78. *That* indicates a restrictive connection; *which* indicates a nonrestrictive. "The river that flows through our ranch . . . ." But, "The Smith Fork, which flows through our ranch . . . ." *Which* is almost always preceded by a comma.

Consistency

79. Avoid "careless shifts in psychic distance," that is, not merely the physical distance between the reader's view and the story, but also his distance from the mind of the character you write about.[148] Give smooth transitions between different perspectives: remote, personal and so on. "Shifts in psychic distance" should be "carefully controlled. At the beginning of the story, in the usual case, we find the writer using either long or medium shots. He moves in a little for scenes of high intensity, draws back for transitions, moves in still closer for the story's climax."[149] This holds for any narrative writing, fact or fiction.

For example, James Joyce's story "The Dead" begins with a long-range shot of a household party, with the maid and guests and hostesses rushing busily around. Finally Gabriel comes; he is the hostesses' favorite nephew, for whom they have been anxiously waiting. The maid takes care of his coat while they talk—a medium shot. Next we see Gabriel by himself—a close-up shot; we hear his thoughts and search his feelings.[150]

Look at the following example of an opening from "A Stroke of Good Fortune" by Flannery O'Connor. The first two sentences show Ruby from some distance as she comes into the apartment lobby. But then we view her from close-up as she looks into the mirror, and we begin to see into her character:

> Ruby came in the front door of the apartment building and lowered the paper sack with the four cans of number three beans in it onto the hall table. She was too tired to take her arms from around it or to straighten up and she hung there collapsed from the hips, her head balanced like a big florid vegetable at the top of the sack. She gazed with stony unrecognition at the face that confronted her in the dark yellow-spotted mirror over the table. Against her right cheek was a gritty collard leaf that had been stuck there half the way home. She gave it a vicious swipe with her arm and straightened up, muttering, "Collards, collards," in a voice of sultry subdued wrath.[151]

Now look at this rewrite of almost the same sentences, only rearranged:

> Ruby came in the front door of the apartment building and lowered the paper sack with the four cans of number three beans in it onto the hall table. She gazed with stony unrecognition at the face that confronted her in the dark yellow-spotted mirror over the table. She was too tired to take her arms from around the package or to straighten up. Against her right cheek was a gritty collard leaf that had been stuck there half the way home. She hung there leaning on the table, collapsed from the hips, her head balanced like a big florid vegetable at the top of the

> sack. She gave the collard leaf a vicious swipe with her arm and straightened up, muttering, "Collards, collards," in a voice of sultry subdued wrath.

Here the reader can hardly keep the continuity because he's jolted back and forth inside Ruby's mind and then outside again in a choppy, confusing manner. The psychic distance constantly shifts back and forth rather than unfolding naturally from remote to near. You *can* move back and forth between different psychic distances, but do it with consistency and so that the reader can see why the shifts take place. The shifts must contribute to the reader's understanding, not disrupt it.

80. Make your viewpoint consistent. Don't shift back and forth between *we* and *you*, or *I* and *he*. If you do need to shift, indicate your shift to the reader with some appropriate signal, such as a hiatus, and then stick consistently with your new viewpoint until that changes.

General Structure

81. When possible, your paragraphs should each be "organized around a single major point."[152] This includes the explanations, examples, elucidations and so on of that point. Try not to pack more than one major point per paragraph, or "your points will tend to get lost, and so will your reader."[153] But remember Baker's balancing comment:

> You have heard that a paragraph is a single idea, and this is true. But so is a word, usually; and so is a sentence, sometimes. It seems best, after all, to think of a paragraph as something you use for your reader's convenience, rather than as some granitic form laid down by molten logic.[154]

With this in mind, don't make paragraphs too long or too short: too long makes writing seem impenetrable; too short makes it appear insubstantial.[155] If your writing becomes impenetrable, your paragraph may be too long. If it lacks substance, maybe your paragraph is too short. Use very short paragraphs only for emphasis and very long ones only to maintain *needed* continuity in the unfolding of a complex idea. Also remember, uniform length produces monotony. "Vary your pacing to keep your piece alive . . . ."[156]

Each paragraph should have cohesion and clarity. Your point should be clear, and all the parts of the paragraph should fit around this point. Just as you build your whole piece of writing around a thesis or premise, so should your paragraph be built around a central "topic." The unifying topic of the paragraph should generally be stated somewhere near the beginning of the paragraph, usually in the first sentence. But whatever else it does, the first sentence in a paragraph must also serve as a "*bridge* . . . whose prime function is to convey the reader over into the new paragraph."[157] This transition function may go together with the stating of your paragraph topic. But you may have to go into your next sentence before you can state the topic. In your first paragraph, you may introduce your thesis for the whole essay or story at the *end* of this paragraph. The earlier material of that paragraph will lead toward the statement of the thesis.

82. In long pieces of writing, "periodically summarize your argument" to help your reader "keep his bearings." You can present such summaries "in the form of brief transitional paragraphs, perhaps only three or four sentences in length."[158]

83. Use chapter breaks, section breaks, hiatuses and so on to help your reader understand and follow your story and explanation.

84. All titles—of your book, essay or story, of chapters or sections—should be succinct, pointed, powerful and, above all, “accurately descriptive (leave the ‘teasing’ title to cute writers).”[159]

Whenever you undertake a radical revision of your writing, keep a copy of the original.[160] Don’t make any of the changes called for on these checklists, even changes in punctuation, mechanically. Remember, what we’ve given here provides only a guideline. Formula cannot substitute for writing.

Notes

1. Jacques Barzun, *Simple and Direct: A Rhetoric for Writers,* rev. ed. (New York: Harper and Row, 1985), p. 14.

2. Ibid., p. 7.

3. Ibid., p. 28.

4. Ibid., p. 11.

5. Ibid., p. 28.

6. Ibid., pp. 28-29.

7. Ibid., p. 29 (emphasis in original).

8. Ibid.

9. Ibid., p. 12.

10. Ibid., p. 30.

11. Ibid., p. 31.

12. Jerome Stern, *Making Shapely Fiction* (New York: W. W. Norton and Co., 1991), p. 102.

13. James J. Kilpatrick, *The Writer's Art* (Kansas City, Kansas: Andrews, McMeel and Parker, 1984), pp. 86-87.

14. John R. Trimble, *Writing with Style: Conversations on the Art of Writing* (Englewood Cliffs, N.J.: Prentice Hall, 1975), pp. 79-80.

15. Pat Kubis and Bob Howland, *Writing Fiction, Nonfiction, and How to Publish* (Reston, Va.: Reston Publishing Co., 1985), p. 206.

16. Trimble, *Writing with Style*, p. 80.

17. Pascal, *Pensées*, trans. A. J. Krailsheimer (1966; reprint, New York: Penguin Books, 1984), p. 64.

18. Barzun, *Simple and Direct*, p. 13.

19. Ibid.

20. Ibid., pp. 13-14.

21. Ibid., p. 20.

22. Ibid., p. 27 (emphasis in original).

23. Ibid.

24. Ibid., p. 18.

25. Kilpatrick, *The Writer's Art*, pp. 77-78.

26. Barzun, *Simple and Direct*, p. 27 (emphasis added).

27. Kubis and Howland, *Writing Fiction, Nonfiction, and How to Publish*, p. 207.

28. Ken Macrorie, *Telling Writing*, 4th ed. (Upper Montclair, N.J.: Boynton/Cook Publishers, 1985), p. 36.

29. Kilpatrick, *The Writer's Art*, pp. 84-86.

30. Kubis and Howland, *Writing Fiction, Nonfiction, and How to Publish*, p. 206.

31. William Strunk, Jr., and E. B. White, *Elements of Style*, 3d ed. (New York: Macmillan, 1979), p. 17.

32. George Orwell, "Politics and the English Language," in *The Modern Stylists: Writers on the Art of Writing*, ed. Donald Hall (New York: Free Press, 1968), p. 22.

33. John Gardner, *The Art of Fiction: Notes on Craft for Young Writers* (New York: Random House, Vintage Books, 1985), p. 99.

34. Ibid., pp. 101-2.

35. Macrorie, *Telling Writing*, p. 89.

36. Barzun, *Simple and Direct*, p. 31.

37. Ibid.

38. Ibid., p. 32.

39. Ibid.

40. Ibid.

41. Ibid.

42. Ibid., p. 33.

43. Ibid., p. 49.

44. John Fairfax and John Moat, *The Way to Write* (New York: St. Martin's Press, 1981), p. 38.

45. Ibid.

46. Ibid.

47. Barzun, *Simple and Direct*, p. 49.

48. Ibid., p. 50.

49. Ibid.

50. Ibid., p. 33.

51. Ibid., pp. 33-34.

52. Ibid., p. 34.

53. Judy Delton, *The 29 Most Common Writing Mistakes and How to Avoid Them* (Cincinnati, Ohio: Writer's Digest Books, 1985), p. 24.

54. Burroway, *Writing Fiction*, p. 87.

55. Ibid.

56. Ibid.

57. Ibid.

58. Kubis and Howland, *Writing Fiction, Nonfiction, and How to Publish*, p. 206.

59. Ibid.

60. Ibid., p. 207.

61. Gardner, *The Art of Fiction*, p. 100.

62. Ibid.

63. Ibid.

64. Ibid.

65. Ibid., p. 101.

66. Ibid.

67. Kilpatrick, *The Writer's Art*, p. 114.

68. Wendell Berry, *The Wild Birds: Six Stories of the Port William Membership* (San Francisco: North Point Press, 1986), pp. 79-80.

69. Wendell Berry, *The Memory of Old Jack* (San Diego, Calif.: A Harvest/HBJ Book, 1974), pp. 4-5.

70. Orson Scott Card, *Characters and Viewpoint* (Cincinnati, Ohio: Writer's Digest Books, 1988), p. 132.

71. Burroway, *Writing Fiction*, p. 269.

72. Jon Franklin, *Writing for Story* (New York: New American Library, Mentor Books, 1987), p. 84.

73. Trimble, *Writing with Style*, p. 79.

74. Ibid.

75. Burroway, *Writing Fiction*, p. 89.

76. Ibid.

77. Kubis and Howland, *Writing Fiction, Nonfiction, and How to Publish*, p. 208.

78. Orwell, "Politics and the English Language," p. 22.

79. Ibid., p. 27.

80. Ibid., p. 22.

81. Barzun, *Simple and Direct*, p. 41.

82. Ibid., p. 17.

83. Ibid.

84. Ibid.

85. Ibid., pp. 17-18.

86. Ibid., pp. 18, 17.

87. Trimble, *Writing with Style*, p. 79.

88. Gardner, *The Art of Fiction*, p. 99.

89. Fairfax and Moat, *The Way to Write*, p. 28 (emphasis in original).

90. Wendell Berry, *A Place on Earth*, rev. ed. (San Francisco: North Point Press, 1983), p. 4.

91. Macrorie, *Telling Writing*, p. 45.

92. Gardner, *The Art of Fiction*, p. 108.

93. Fairfax and Moat, *The Way to Write*, pp. 69-70.

94. Ibid., p. 70.

95. Ibid., p. 68.

96. Ibid., p. 69.

97. Macrorie, *Telling Writing*, p. 36.

98. Hall, *The Modern Stylists*, p. 27.

99. Claire Kehrwald Cook, *Line by Line: How to Improve Your Own Writing* (Boston: Houghton Mifflin, 1985), p. 5.

100. Strunk and White, *The Elements of Style*, p. 18.

101. Joseph M. Williams, *Style: Ten Lessons in Clarity and Grace* (Glenview, Ill.: Scott, Foresman and Co., 1981), p. 33.

102. Ibid., p. 32.

103. Ibid., p. 33.

104. Ibid., pp. 32-33.

105. Ibid., p. 33.

106. Ibid., p. 34.

107. Ibid., p. 38.

108. Ibid.

109. Robert Graves and Alan Hodge, *The Reader over Your Shoulder: A Handbook for Writers of English Prose*, 2d ed. (New York: Vintage Books, 1979), p. 160.

110. Robert Scholes and Carl H. Klaus, *Elements of Writing* (New York: Oxford University Press, 1972), pp. 12-13.

111. Gardner, *The Art of Fiction*, p. 99.

112. Kilpatrick, *The Writer's Art*, p. 114, quoting Douglas Southall Freeman.

113. Gardner, *The Art of Fiction*, p. 104.

114. Ibid.

115. Ibid., p. 99.

116. Ibid.

117. Ernest Hemingway, *The Old Man and the Sea* (New York: Bantam Books, 1952), pp. 105-6.

118. Harry Levin, ed., *The Portable James Joyce* (New York: Viking Press, 1975), p. 213.

119. Kilpatrick, *The Writer's Art*, p. 114, quoting Douglas Southall Freeman (emphasis in original).

120. Ibid. (emphasis in original).

121. Ibid.

122. Stern, *Making Shapely Fiction*, p. 101.

123. Strunk and White, *The Elements of Style*, p. 17.

124. Trimble, *Writing with Style*, p. 55, quoting F. L. Lucas.

125. Donald Murray, *Writing for Your Readers: Notes on the Writer's Craft from* The Boston Globe (Chester, Conn.: Globe Pequot Press, 1983), p. 73.

126. Ibid., p. 74.

127. Strunk and White, *The Elements of Style*, pp. 19-20.

128. Ibid., p. 20.

129. Gardner, *The Art of Fiction*, p. 114.

130. Ibid., p. 115.

131. Ibid.

132. Ibid., p. 117.

133. Ibid.

134. Ibid., p. 118.

135. Ibid.

136. Ibid., p. 119.

137. Ansen Dibell, *Plot* (Cincinnati, Ohio: Writer's Digest Books, 1988), p. 7.

138. Ibid., p. 81.

139. Ibid., p. 82.

140. C. Hugh Holman and William Harmon, *A Handbook to Literature*, 5th ed. (New York: Macmillan, 1986), p. 295.

141. Gardner, *The Art of Fiction*, p. 119.

142. Ibid., pp. 120-21.

143. Alexander Cockburn, "Heatherdown: A Late Imperialist Memoir," in *The Best American Essays 1986*, ed. Elizabeth Harwick and

Robert Atwan (New York: Ticknor and Fields, 1986), pp. 77-78.

144. *Webster's New World Dictionary*, 2d college ed., s.v. "ersatz."

145. Trimble, *Writing with Style*, p. 51.

146. Ibid.

147. Ibid., p. 52.

148. Gardner, *The Art of Fiction*, p. 99.

149. Ibid., p. 112.

150. Levin, *The Portable James Joyce*, pp. 190-95.

151. Flannery O'Connor, "A Stroke of Good Fortune," in *A Good Man Is Hard to Find and Other Stories* (San Diego, Calif.: Harcourt Brace Jovanovich, A Harvest/HBJ Book, 1983), p. 69.

152. Trimble, *Writing with Style*, p. 53.

153. Ibid., p. 54.

154. Sheridan Baker, *The Practical Stylist*, 6th ed. (New York: Harper and Row, 1985), p. 41.

155. Trimble, *Writing with Style*, p. 81.

156. Ibid.

157. Ibid., p. 54.

158. Ibid., p. 80.

159. Ibid., p. 81.

160. Burroway, *Writing Fiction*, p. 39.

Bibliography

Books

Baker, Sheridan. *The Practical Stylist.* 6th ed. New York: Harper and Row, 1985.

Barzun, Jacques. *Simple and Direct: A Rhetoric for Writers.* rev. ed. New York: Harper and Row, 1985.

Berry, Wendell. *The Memory of Old Jack.* San Diego, Calif.: Harcourt Brace Jovanovich, A Harvest/HBJ Book, 1974.

_____. *A Place on Earth.* rev. ed. San Francisco: North Point Press, 1983.

_____. *The Wild Birds: Six Stories of the Port William Membership.* San Francisco: North Point Press, 1986.

Burroway, Janet. *Writing Fiction: A Guide to Narrative Craft.* 2d ed. Boston: Little, Brown and Co., 1987.

Card, Orson Scott. *Characters and Viewpoint.* Cincinnati, Ohio: Writer's Digest Books, 1988.

Cook, Claire Kehrwald. *Line by Line: How to Improve Your Own Writing.* Boston: Houghton Mifflin, 1985.

Delton, Judy. *The 29 Most Common Writing Mistakes and How to Avoid Them.* Cincinnati, Ohio: Writer's Digest Books, 1985.

Dibell, Ansen. *Plot.* Cincinnati, Ohio: Writer's Digest Books, 1988.

Fairfax, John, and John Moat. *The Way to Write.* New York: St. Martin's Press, 1981.

Franklin, Jon. *Writing for Story.* New York: New American Library, Mentor Books, 1987.

Gardner, John. *The Art of Fiction: Notes on Craft for Young Writers.* New York: Random House, Vintage Books, 1985.

Graves, Robert, and Alan Hodge. *The Reader over Your Shoulder: A Handbook for Writers of English Prose.* 2d ed. New York: Random House, Vintage Books, 1979.

Hall, Donald, ed. *The Modern Stylists: Writers on the Art of Writing.* New York: Free Press, 1968.

Hemingway, Ernest. *The Old Man and the Sea.* New York: Bantam

Books, 1952.

Holman, C. Hugh, and William Harmon. *A Handbook to Literature.* 5th ed. New York: Macmillan Publishing Co., 1986.

Joyce, James. *The Portable James Joyce.* Edited by Harry Levin. New York: Viking Press, 1981.

Kilpatrick, James J. *The Writer's Art.* Kansas City, Kansas: Andrews, McMeel and Parker, 1984.

Kubis, Pat, and Bob Howland. *Writing Fiction, Nonfiction, and How to Publish.* Reston, Va.: Reston Publishing Co., 1985.

Macrorie, Ken. *Telling Writing.* 4th ed. Upper Montclair, N.J.: Boynton/Cook Publishers, 1985.

Murray, Donald. *Writing for Your Readers: Notes on the Writer's Craft from* The Boston Globe. *Chester, Conn.: Globe Pequot Press, 1983.*

O'Connor, Flannery. *A Good Man Is Hard to Find.* San Diego: A Harvest/HBJ Book, 1954.

Pascal. *Pensées.* Translated by A. J. Krailsheimer. 1966. Reprint. New York: Penguin Books, 1984.

Scholes, Robert, and Carl H. Klaus. *Elements of Writing.* New York: Oxford University Press, 1972.

Stern, Jerome. *Making Shapely Fiction.* New York: W. W. Norton and Co., 1991.

Strunk, William Jr., and E. B. White. *The Elements of Style.* 3d ed. New York: Macmillan Publishing, 1979.

Trimble, John R. *Writing with Style: Conversations on the Art of Writing.* Englewood Cliffs, N.J.: Prentice-Hall, 1975.

Williams, Joseph M. *Style: Ten Lessons in Clarity and Grace.* Glenview, Ill.: Scott, Foresman and Co., 1981.

Articles

Cockburn, Alexander. "Heatherdown: A Late Imperialist Memoir." In *The Best American Essays 1986,* edited by Elizabeth Hardwick and Robert Atwan. New York: Ticknor and Fields, 1986.

Orwell, George. "Politics and the English Language." In *The Modern Stylists: Writers on the Art of Writing,* edited by Donald Hall. New York: Free Press, 1968.